WHERE DO I BURY THIS LOVE

AKSHAT THAPA

i

Copyright © <2025><Akshat Thapa >

.To the ones who loved deeply but lost silently.

To the hearts that still whisper names long forgotten by the world.

To the souls who carry the weight of unsaid goodbyes and unreturned love.

This book is for you—the ones who tread between hope and heartbreak, who still hold onto echoes, who have learned that some ghosts are not meant to be forgotten, only carried.

May these words find you in the quiet hours, where love lingers and longing never truly fades.

Foreword

There are emotions too heavy for words, yet too restless for silence. Love, longing, grief, and hope—they weave themselves into the quiet corners of our hearts, demanding to be felt, even when we try to forget.

This book is not just a collection of poems and thoughts; it is a journey through the ruins of love and the echoes of what remains. It speaks to the nights spent missing someone who no longer calls your name, the weight of words left unspoken, and the fragile hope that lingers even in the darkest hours.

Each poem, each line, is a fragment of something larger—an unfinished conversation, an unsent letter, a dream that never became reality. Some will find sorrow in these pages; others will find healing. Perhaps you will find both, because isn't that what love is? A beautiful ache, a wound that never fully closes, a hope that refuses to die.

If you have ever loved and lost, if you have ever held on to a memory long after it faded, this book is for you. Let these words be a companion to your quiet moments, a reminder that you are not alone in what you feel.

— **akshat thapa**

Preface

Love and loss are not opposites; they are two sides of the same aching truth. To love is to risk breaking, and to lose is to carry the weight of what once was, forever imprinted on the soul. This book is born from that delicate space between holding on and letting go, between longing for the past and hoping for tomorrow.

Each poem and thought within these pages is an echo of emotions too heavy to be spoken aloud, yet too powerful to be ignored. They are for the ones who still feel the warmth of hands they can no longer hold, who still hear voices in the silence, who still search for pieces of themselves in the memories of another.

This is not just a collection of words—it is a home for those who have loved deeply and lost silently. It is for those who carry unfinished goodbyes in their hearts, who know that sometimes, the deepest grief is not in losing someone, but in knowing they still exist somewhere, just not with you.

If these pages make you pause, if they make you remember, if they make you feel—then they have done what they were meant to do. This book is yours now. May you find in it a reflection of your own heart, and

perhaps, the courage to embrace both the beauty and
the pain of what it means to love.

Acknowledgments

This book is a collection of emotions too raw to be spoken, too heavy to be forgotten. It exists because of the love, loss, and longing that have shaped me—and for that, I have many to thank.

To the ones who stayed, and to the ones who left—thank you. You have been the ink in these pages, the echoes behind every word. Some of you remain as warm hands in the present, while others exist only as ghosts in my memories. Either way, you have left your mark, and this book would not have been written without you.

To the hearts that have known love in its most beautiful and most painful forms—this is for you. Your silent battles, your unspoken grief, and your quiet hopes have breathed life into these words. If you have ever felt the ache of missing someone who no longer belongs to your world, know that you are not alone.

To my readers—thank you for carrying these words with you. If they bring you comfort, if they stir something within you, if they remind you that love, even when lost, is never truly gone—then this book has found its purpose.

And lastly, to love itself—the kind that stays, the kind that leaves, and the kind that lingers long after it's gone. You have been my greatest teacher, my deepest sorrow, and my most enduring hope.

ACKNOWLEDGMENTS

With gratitude and heart

Introduction

Love is not always a gentle whisper—it is sometimes a storm that leaves us shattered, a shadow that lingers even after the light has gone. This book is a collection of those moments, where love meets longing, where hope and heartbreak intertwine, and where silence speaks louder than words.

We often believe that love is only real when it is whole, when it is reciprocated, when it lasts forever. But what about the love that lingers in empty spaces? The kind that stays even when the person is gone? The love that exists in unsent messages, in familiar songs, in places we can no longer visit without feeling the weight of a memory? That love is just as real—perhaps even more so.

Each poem in these pages is a quiet confession, a piece of a heart left behind in words. Some will remind you of what you have lost, others will remind you of what you still carry. If you have ever held on too tightly, or let go too late—these words are for you.

This book is not just poetry; it is a mirror for those who have felt deeply and lost silently. It is a reminder that even in the deepest sorrow, hope still flickers. That love, in all its forms—whether whole, broken, or unfinished— never truly disappears.

So read these words slowly. Let them sink into the quiet parts of your heart. And perhaps, somewhere between the lines, you will find yourself

The weight of silence

The walls have learned to whisper,
where your voice once used to be.
They hum in hushed tones,
echoing laughter now faded,
carrying the ghosts of words unspoken.

> They do not know your name anymore,
> only the absence you left behind.
> They hold shadows instead of memories,
> a silence so heavy it bends the air,
> a quiet so loud it drowns me.

The sound of a name unspoken

Your name still rests on my lips,
a syllable away from breaking,
fragile as glass, trembling,
shaped by breath but never spoken.

I have swallowed it so many times,
let it settle in my ribs like a buried secret,
let it carve itself into the hollow of my chest,
where it lingers—aching, pulsing, waiting.

A love that never arrived

I set the table for two,
knowing well you will not come.
Still, I lay out the silverware,
still, I light the candle,
as if habit could conjure your presence,
as if longing could rewrite fate.

I pour the wine,
watch the glass catch the glow of the flame,
and wonder—if hope were strong enough,
would it pull you back through the door?

Or am I only toasting to a love
that never learned how to stay?

The last page

I turned the page to find an ending
I never saw coming.
The ink smudged, the story torn—
a chapter stolen by silence.

Some stories do not fade—
they are torn away, mid-sentence,
leaving only unfinished echoes,
words stranded in the margins,
a final goodbye that never arrived.

And so, I trace the last line again,
searching for closure in the space between words,
but all I find is the weight of what was left unsaid.

A House Without Footsteps

The floorboards no longer creak
under the weight of your laughter.
The air does not carry your voice,
does not hold the warmth of your breath.

This house is not empty,
but it no longer feels like home.
The walls stand just the same,
yet they ache with something missing,
with a silence that does not belong.

I walk through rooms still filled with you,
but all that lingers is the shape of loss,
woven into the spaces you used to fill.

when love become a ghost

You still live here, in the shadows of my mind,
soft footsteps in the quiet,
a whisper where your name used to be.

I do not speak to you anymore,
but that does not stop you from answering.
Your voice lingers in the hush of dusk,
your touch in the cold of an empty bed.

Some loves do not leave—
they fade into the corners of memory,
haunting, lingering, waiting to be remembered.

The thing we could not say

Not all words need to be spoken
for silence to wound like a knife.
Not every scream is born of sound—
some live in the spaces between breath.

The things we never said
still sit between us like ghosts,
looming, whispering, unravelling.
And though our lips remained sealed,
our silence still found a way to shatter us.

A letter without an address

I write to you in the margins of my mind,
letters that will never find their way.
Each word, a confession too heavy to carry aloud,
each sentence, an echo of what could have been.

The ink bleeds like longing,
the paper wears the weight of regret.
Still, I write, knowing well
you will never read the things
I am too afraid to say aloud.

If time had a heart 

Would time take back the seconds it stole?
Would it gather the moments it shattered,
piece them together like mended glass?

Would it return the love it erased,
undo the spaces where goodbyes took root?
Or does time only know how to steal,
how to carry memories away
without a glance in the rearview mirror?

The shape of you're absence

You are gone,
but the spaces you filled still whisper your name.
The chair you once sat in sighs beneath my touch,
the doorframe still carries the shadow of your laughter.

Your absence is not empty—
it is vast, endless,
a shape carved into the air,
a presence in the quiet,
a love that lingers in the spaces you left behind.

where we left   off

I still walk the streets we claimed as ours,
where laughter once echoed between us,
where our footsteps danced in rhythm,
where time seemed to pause just for us.

Half-expecting to find you waiting,
half-dreading that I won't.
At the corner where we last parted,
the wind carries your absence like a whisper,
and I stand still—unsure if I should move forward,
or turn back toward a past I can no longer reach.

The ocean knows

I have told the waves about you,
let them carry your name into the horizon,
where the sky meets the sea in an endless embrace.

And they return to me softer each time,
as if the tide understands longing,
as if the ocean itself has learned
to miss someone who will never return.

A love that was almost real

Perhaps we were never meant to last,
like a sunset that vanishes too soon,
or a melody that lingers
long after the song has ended.

But for a moment,
you made me believe we could,
and maybe that was enough—
to taste love, even if it never stayed,
to hold something fleeting,
and call it real for just a little while.

Between the Lines of a Forgotten Poem

I have searched old notebooks for pieces of you,
for the words we once breathed into existence,
for the verses that held your laughter,
for the lines where your love still lived.

But the ink has faded faster than my memories,
leaving only empty spaces
where we used to be.
And I wonder—
did we write our love too lightly,
or was it never meant to last on paper at all?

If we had more time

Would you have stayed
if the world had given us just one more day?
Would we have walked slower,
savoured each moment,
held onto each other just a little longer?

Would your hands have lingered in mine,
would your eyes have said what your lips never could?
Or was time never the enemy—
was it always just us,
running out of reasons to hold on?

The Spaces Between Our Fingers

Your hands fit mine like a promise,
a perfect match in a fleeting moment,
as if the universe had designed us to belong—
even if only for a while.

But some promises are never meant to be kept,
some hands are not meant to hold forever.
And now, the spaces between my fingers
feel like echoes of you,
a silent reminder of something once whole,
now missing.

The Kiss We Never Had

Sometimes, the most beautiful things
are the ones that never happened—
the almost-touch, the unspoken words,
the love that lived in glances, not in lips.

Perhaps we were meant to remain unfinished,
a story left in the hands of imagination,
a dream sweeter than reality could ever be.
For what is untouched cannot be broken,
and maybe that is why
you and I remain something close to perfect.

The Love That Lingers

Not all love disappears.
Some stay, even when the people do not.
It lingers in forgotten songs,
in the scent of a season,
in a place that suddenly feels familiar.
It waits in quiet moments,
in echoes of laughter,
in the spaces where we thought love had left.
But love never truly leaves—
it just finds new ways to remind us
it was once here.

A Poem for the One Who Left

I do not write to bring you back.
I know love cannot reverse time,
nor can words summon ghosts.

I write to remember what it felt like
when you were here,
to hold onto the warmth
of what is now only a memory.

These lines are not for you,
but for the version of me
that once loved you—
so that I may remind myself
that love was real,
even when you are not.

The Moment Before the Fall

There was a moment—
right before the sky collapsed,
before love unravelled at the seams,
before goodbye became the only word left—

where I swore you looked at me
like I was something real,
like I was something worth holding onto.

And for that single breath,
I let myself believe it too.
But moments are not forever,
and neither were we.

When Shadows Hold Hands

I have danced with my own darkness
for far too long,
letting the echoes of old pain
twist into lullabies,
singing me into sleepless nights.

But tonight, I let the stars cut in—
they take my trembling hands,
guiding me back to the light.
They whisper that even the lost
can learn to glow again.

The Night I Stopped Calling Your Name

Healing is not sudden.
It does not arrive in grand gestures
or epiphanies at dawn.

It happens in the quiet moments—
the day your name feels more like a memory
than a wound,
when the sound of it no longer aches,
when I whisper it just to see
if it still holds weight—
and find that it doesn't.

If You Leave, Leave Gently

If you must go,
do not slam the door.
Do not let your absence
echo like a final, cruel note
in a song unfinished.

Let the silence settle softly,
like the hush of waves pulling back,
like footprints fading in the tide.
If you must go,
leave gently,
so I can learn to stand
without the weight of your ghost.

A Love Letter to Tomorrow

Dear tomorrow,
I have spent too long mourning yesterday,
tracing the past with shaking hands,
as if I could rewrite it.

But today,
I raise my head to meet you.
I stand at the edge of possibility,
unafraid, unburdened.

Dear tomorrow,
I am ready to begin again.

The Light That Remains

Even after the fire dies,
after the last ember is swallowed by night,
after the warmth is only a memory—
a little heat still lingers in the ashes.

Love does not vanish all at once.
It stays in the spaces between,
in the places we least expect.
Even when the fire is gone,
there is still light to be found.

The Day I Stopped Waiting

One morning, I woke up
and the air felt lighter,
as if I had exhaled you in my sleep.

The space beside me did not ache,
the clock did not mock me,
the door did not hold its breath.

And that is how I knew—
I no longer needed you to return.

When the Light Breaks Through

Even the longest nights end.
Even the stars, once swallowed by darkness,
return to paint the sky.

Even the broken find their way home—
not in a rush, not all at once,
but step by step, breath by breath,
with light seeping through the cracks,
showing them the way.

The Quiet Strength of Letting Go....

Letting go is not weakness.
It is not surrender.
It is standing at the edge of the past,
choosing not to jump.

It is the silent courage of moving forward,
the quiet decision to love yourself more,
to walk away without looking back,
to trust that there is something ahead
worth reaching for.

The Road to Something New

Healing is not a straight path.
It twists, it turns,
it circles back when you least expect.

Some days, you will feel whole.
Other days, you will ache again.
But every step forward,
no matter how small,
is still progress.

And one day,
you will look back and realize—
you made it.>>3

The Sun Still Rises

Even when the night seems endless,
when the weight of darkness presses in,
when the stars flicker like dying embers—

the sun finds its way home.
It pushes through the horizon,
a quiet promise written in gold,
whispering, *hold on just a little longer.*

Because no matter how long the night lingers,
morning always finds a way back.

The Moon Watches Over the Lonely

You are never truly alone.
Even when the world turns its back,
when voices fade into silence,
when your own thoughts feel too loud—

look up.

The moon has been watching over you all along,
a quiet companion in the emptiness,
glowing softly in the dark,
reminding you that even in solitude,
you are seen.

A New Beginning in Disguise

Some endings arrive like storms—
loud, merciless, tearing through everything
you thought was unshakable.

But not all destruction is ruin.
Sometimes, the wreckage is just space
being cleared for something better.

Some endings are just beginnings
we do not yet understand.

The Courage to Stay Soft

It takes strength to remain kind
in a world that has tried to harden you,
to let your heart remain open
when it has been shattered before.

But softness is not weakness—
it is a quiet rebellion,
a refusal to become bitter,
a decision to keep loving
despite the reasons not to.

The Beauty of Being Found

You have spent so long
hiding behind quiet smiles,
waiting for someone to notice
the light you carry inside.

One day, someone will see you
the way you always wished to be seen.
Not just in glimpses,
not just in passing,
but fully—
as if you were never invisible at all.

The Love That Comes After Loss

Even after everything is gone,
when the echoes of goodbye still linger,
when the world feels colder, emptier—

love still finds a way to return.
It comes in unfamiliar forms,
in places you never thought to look—
a kind word, a stranger's smile,
the warmth of the sun on your skin.

It does not replace what was lost,
but it reminds you that love never truly leaves.

A Home Within Yourself

You are not lost.
You are simply learning
how to be your own home.

To sit with yourself in silence
and not feel alone.
To embrace your own heart
like an old friend returning.

You are not a wanderer without a place.
You are a universe within yourself,
and that is enough.

Laughter in an Empty Room

Even after the people leave,
after the doors close
and the dust begins to settle,
the love they brought never truly disappears.

It lingers in the walls,
in the quiet corners of memory,
in the way the air still hums
with the laughter that once filled it.

Some things do not fade.
Some things stay—
even when we cannot see them.

What If Happiness Is Just Ahead?

You have spent so long
looking for it behind you,
digging through old days,
searching for something to hold onto.

But what if happiness is not in the past?
What if it is waiting just beyond tomorrow?
What if it is standing right ahead,
arms open, ready to be found—
if only you take the step forward?

The Art of Beginning Again

It's never too late to rewrite the story.
To turn the page,
to start fresh,
to pick up the pen and say,
I will not let this be the end.

You are not bound by past chapters,
not defined by the things that broke you.
You are still here,
still breathing,
still capable of writing something beautiful—
something new

The hardest goodbyes are the ones never said, just felt in the way someone stops trying…….

We didn't end in a fight, or with words—we just became strangers with memories

I act like I don't care, but deep down, I wonder if you
ever think of me too

One day, I'll stop checking if you saw my message…
and that's when you'll miss me

I stopped talking about it, not because I moved on, but because no one ever really listened………. 💔

I hate that I can't hate you, even after all the ways you made me feel unwanted

I stayed up all night overthinking, while you slept peacefully, never even thinking of me.......

You broke my heart, but I still flinch at the thought of you being hurt...

It hurts when you realize you meant nothing to someone
who meant everything to you

You replaced me so easily, and I'm still here, trying to forget how it felt to be yours…………...